If You Were Me and Lived in...
the Middle Ages

By Carole P. Roman

Illustrated by Mateya Arkova

For my grandparents and family, who never had a chance to tell their stories.

Special thanks to my daughter-in-law, Sharon, who always helps me look good!

Copyright 2015 Carole P. Roman All rights reserved.
ISNB-10: 1-947118-57-9 ISBN-13: 978-1-947118-57-7
Library of Congress Control Number: 2012921018
CreateSpace Independent Publishing Platform,
North Charleston, SC

If you were me and lived in the Middle Ages, you would have been born about the year 1072, more than 900 years ago.

This is what a small town in England looks like now.

This is what a rural village might have looked like at the end of the first millennium.

Historians like to call this time period the Medieval (Mid-e-vil) or Middle Ages. The Medieval time period officially began roughly in the late 400s and lasted until the Renaissance (Ren-ai-san-ce) in the early 1400s.

The Roman Empire controlled most of Europe. It was famous for its strong network of safe roads, coinage, and a stable government that was defended by a vast and powerful army. This encouraged trade and the exchange of ideas between regions.

In 476, the Roman Empire fell apart, extinguishing communication and fracturing Europe into small communities called feudal (few-dal) holdings that were governed by princes or warlords. Feudalism (few-dal-ism) divided the vast empire into small kingdoms.

Each of the rulers of these small territories or fiefdoms (feef-doms) held control of all the money and people who lived and worked the land.

They needed private soldiers to help them protect their holdings. Trained warriors called knights sold their services. Often they were given land as payment. They became vassals (vass-uhls) to the person ruling the area. This meant they owed all their loyalty to the prince or warlord and would defend and fight for him.

The land attached to the castle or manor house was called a demesne (dea-meyn).

The land was worked by peasants living there. These peasants were farmers called serfs and they were given small plots to farm, feed and support the manor or castle. There were two types of serfs: free and un-free.

The main difference between these two types of peasants was land.

A lord owned everything from animals to clothes with an un-free serf. They were forbidden to leave the manor and had little for themselves.

Free peasants owned their farm and could carry a weapon. Either way, it was long hours with little reward and crippling taxes. All serfs owed services to their liege (lee-je) or lord. This leader dictated most of the rules and had control of what the serfs did in most of their daily life.

If you were a boy during this time in history, your name could have been Geoffrey (Jef-free) or Roul (Ro-ul).

Aalis (A-lish) or Melisende (Me-le-sand) were popular girls' names. In fact, your own name was Aalis. You were named after your godmother.

Your family originally lived near a town in France called Rouen (Ro-yhn), so your father was known as Theobald de Rouen (Thee-o-bald de Ro-uhn).

You were called Norman because your family came from Normandy. Some said the people of Normandy were descendants of the Norsemen and Viking (Vyk-ing) explorers from Scandinavia.

Your father was a knight or soldier in William of Normandy's army and was given a large reward for helping when William invaded England.

William the Conqueror became King William the I of England. Your father was a standard bearer which meant he had the important job of carrying and keeping the flag safe during the battle of Hastings in 1066. He has to make sure it was visible for all the troops because as long as they could see their flag, they continued fighting.

For doing this, he was given a piece of land called a demesne that was to provide an income for his family.

Farmers rented land from him and had to give him a large portion of their crops. Your father, in return, had the job to keep them safe. If the king needed your father's support, he had to bring troops to fight for him. He was encouraged to build a big home on the property.

Your father built a large house made out of stone called a motte (mott) and bailey (bail-lee) castle on an man-made hill so it was safe from attackers.

The motte was the raised mound and the bailey was the walled yard where supplies and animals were kept safe. The whole wall was surrounded by a ditch filled with water called a moat. This protected your family from enemies.

There was a gatehouse and drawbridge with many arrow slits in the walls so your father could defend your home if he was attacked. The gatehouse had an iron gate called a portcullis (port-kul-is) that was raised to allow people to enter.

He had permission to crenellate (kren-el-late) the top of the building directly from the king, which meant he built a scalloped outline on the roof, so archers could keep enemies away.

Your family made their home in the part of the castle called the keep. It was a big stone tower. You lived there with all your brothers and sisters, as well as many servants.

Your father wanted to show his new status as a landowner and constructed a comfortable and impressive castle.

It had a great hall in the center with a kitchen and buttery (but-uh-ree) where all the barrels of wine and ale were stored on one side of the building. A chapel to pray in was on the other side of the structure. There was a brewhouse to prepare the ale and a bake house for making bread, as well as a large stable for the horses.

A large kitchen garden was outside where fresh vegetables were grown and tended by the cook. A lovely fish pond was on the property where your brothers fished.

You loved to sit in the large circular building called a dovecote (dove-coat). Doves like to nest there. Every few weeks, one of the servant boys climbed the walls, stealing the young birds for tasty meals for the cook to prepare.

The great hall was located in the center of the home. It was a huge room with a high ceiling where everybody ate and met.

At both ends of this great hall, there was a large fireplace with a chimney to carry out the smoke.

You knew that the fact that you had two chimneys indicated that your family was wealthy.

Windows were small spaces covered by linen soaked in tallow, so they were slightly translucent. This meant they let in little light but kept out the rain.

At night, the servants slept on the floor in the great room on piles of straw.

Your father had been married three times. His first wife died when she had a baby and your own mother when she got sick this past winter. He had six children between both wives. He married your new mother a few weeks ago. She had four children from her first marriage, so now you had nine brothers and sisters.

Your father and step-mother slept in a room right above the great room. This was called a solar (so-ler), and he had a huge bed surrounded by curtains to keep out the drafts. The frame was covered with no less than three different mattresses. First was straw, then wool fleece, and finally a mattress stuffed with goose feathers. They had a fluffy blanchette (blanch-et) draped across it. It was an undyed wool blanket that was expensive and warm.

This was his private room, and no one was allowed there except for family. You sewed every afternoon with your sisters. There was a window where you could watch the knights practicing their skills in the tiltyard. They exercised their horses, practiced swordplay, and did target shooting with a crossbow. They made you feel safe.

There was a fireplace and beautiful tapestries brought all the way from a town called Arras (Ar-rahs) in France.

The tapestries were woven pictures that hung on the walls and kept the drafts out. They were as colorful as they were beautiful. You loved to stare at the handsome men and lovely ladies in all their finery in the pictures.

You enjoyed working there because it was quieter than any other place in the house and out of the way from all the activity. You could sew, talk, and pray in peace.

There were plenty of stools and benches for sitting; a large chest came with your step-mother from her home when she married your father. The solar had a large table where you could all sit and gossip.

The garderobe was where you went to ... well... you know. It was a chute built into the wall with a stone seat. Your father designed it to empty right into the moat!

You took all your meals in the great room with the many people who lived and worked near your home.

Your father, step-mother, and your two oldest brothers sat on a raised platform called a dais so everybody could see them.

Less important people sat at the end or below the salt.

Salt was an important and expensive item. It was extracted from seawater by evaporation and only the rich could afford it.

Nobles sat at the higher tables nearer to the precious salt. It was often called "white gold." Many say that is where the expression "he is worth his salt" came.

You sat near your parents and closer to the salt, indicating you were more important than other people in the household.

You ate well. There was always beef, mutton, pork, and venison on the table. Your cook made all kinds of birds, including swans, ducks, heron, blackbirds, and pigeons.

You used only knives and spoons, and your cup was made from an animal's horn.

The church demanded that Wednesday, Friday, and Saturday were fast days so you were not allowed to eat meat. Those days pike and carp were on the menu.

Your home was famous for the ale they brewed. Sometimes they mixed it with honey. It was called mead. The honey came from bee hives that were kept near the castle's garden.

The kitchen was the busiest place in the castle and was filled with lots of servants. Everyday the cook prepared two major meals for hundreds of people.

Your cook made the meals in a large caldron over an open fire. She wrapped up different foods like eggs, bacon, vegetables, and puddings in cloth bags and placed them in boiling water in the big pot.

She roasted meat in a large fireplace with a spit. A boy called a turnbrocie (turn-bro-cee) constantly turned the slab of meat so that it roasted evenly. The fireplace was big, so he could stand in a part of it while the meat was cooking. Smaller spits cooked ducks, chickens, geese, swans, and doves.

The kitchen smelled of the tasty meat pies and breads baking in the brick ovens. It was always hot in the kitchen; you could barely stand to be in there for a minute.

Your step-mother insisted you understand how the food was prepared; she made you help with the daily menu.

Fish, herbs, and cured ham hung from the ceiling where they dried and could be used in the tasty dishes.

You stopped taking breakfast recently to show how you had grown up. Only weak women and children ate something in the morning. Most people did not eat until dinner.

Dinner was mid-morning and supper at five in the afternoon.

Your meal was served on a large piece of bread called a trencher. It soaked up the juices and afterward was given out to the poor to eat.

You knew that peasants were lucky if they had the occasional rabbit. Mostly they ate dark, coarse bread, and cheese. They ate only one cooked meal a day. It was in the evening and often grain mixed with hot water. Vegetables were thrown in, and it was called a pottage (pot-idge). Often they went hungry, and if food was scarce, they could starve.

Your father wore linen underpants called braies (bray-es). They were knee length and secured around his waist with a belt called a braiel (bray-el). You knew that is where he attached the pouch that held his money.

His legs were covered by woolen hose pulled up and tied to his braies. They had a strap under the arch of his foot to hold them in place, but they were bulky and bunched terribly.

Over that was a linen tunic (too-nick) that fell to his knees. The linen was useful in absorbing his sweat and easier to clean than the woolen tunic he wore over it. Short trousers made from leather ended at his knee. He added a leather belt at his waist.

In the winter, he had a short fur-trimmed cloak called a mantle. The skin side faced outward; the warm squirrel fur was against his clothes. It opened at the right shoulder, so his sword arm was free. A single circular pin made from horn held it in place. It had an amber stone in it which made it valuable. Once he attached the brooch, he never took it off and always slipped the cloak over his head.

He owned a new waist-length coat called a jacket. It had a large collar and made him look important. He was the only man in the village to own one.

Your brothers were dressed the same way as your father.

Their boots were leather with pointed toes and secured with straps. They had warm hats shaped with a point, and your step-mother knitted them gloves in the winter.

Your family was dressed better than the farmers who worked the land. They wore linen tunics and cut up blankets as leggings. Most of them wore woolen cloaks.

In battle, your father wore chain mail to protect his body from swords. It was called a hauberk (haw-berk) and was a shirt made out of small linked metal loops that prevented him from being hurt. He had a kite-shaped shield. He had a pointed top helmet and a tall sword.

You were dressed much like your step-mother. You wore a linen under shift with long, narrow sleeves and a simple long wool dress over it. The sleeves on this overdress were fuller, and the gown itself was colored in a wide variety of dyes from blue to yellow. Contrasting colors were often used on the cuffs and hem. The dresses were ankle length. A fabric sash suspended at the hips held household items like keys or decorative items.

Your step-mother had many pretty brooches. She used them to hold up her dress in the old style.

You knew you had one put aside for when you married. It was your mother's.

Since you were almost thirteen, you knew a marriage was coming soon. Your father was talking to a neighbor about a marriage between you and his brother. You thought he was old and ugly. You wished they would marry you to his son, who was nearer to your age.

You and all the other women wore veils with headbands and cowls (couls). Sometimes, your step-mother wore a barbette (bar-bet), which was a chin strap that wrapped around her chin to hold her veil in place. You preferred to wear a chaplet (chap-lit) which was a wreath of flowers.

It was immodest to show your hair, which you kept braided underneath a veil.

You wore flat-soled leather boots that tied with a flap at the ankle and dyed in many different colors.

Your step-mother's cloak was richly embroidered with gold wires and fur. You and your sister's cloaks were rather plain. The wool was heavy in the summer and made you uncomfortable. Sometimes the fabric was so scratchy it irritated your skin. Your step-mother used herbs from the garden to make a soothing salve for you.

When you left the castle, you wore wooden shoes called pattens (pat-tens). You slipped them on over your regular shoes to protect them from the mud and dirt.

You understood you had a privileged place in society. It wasn't long ago that your father was nothing more than a landless knight.

Through a father owed land, only his older brother would inherit it, just as your oldest brother would inherit the home you were living on now.

One of your younger brothers and little sister would be joining the church. He was to be a priest and she a nun.

Your middle brother was training to be a knight. He intended to join the Crusaders (Kroo-sae-ders) traveling to the Holy Land to protect travelers going on pilgrimages to visit religious sites.

Religion was important in all aspects of your life. You prayed five times a day.

You and your brothers and sisters saw little of your parents. Your brothers were sent to live with a noble family when they were seven years old. This was called fostering. It was a chance for your brothers to learn new things and make valuable friendships for the family.

They started out as a page, basically running errands and acting as a sort of personal servant to a knight. At fourteen, they became a squire (skwire), and they learned how to take care of all the armor and equipment as well as the horses. At twenty-one, they would become a knight, usually by proving his skills or participating in battle.

There was a big ceremony where they would be dubbed, which meant a senior knight would tap their shoulders with a sword while they kneeled at his feet and swore absolute loyalty.

This was an important rite of passage and took years of learning to fight and joust (jou-st) outside in the tiltyard.

Knights wore a suit of armor and held a long lance. They would have to try and unseat another rider with the lance. It was dangerous but a necessary part of life.

There were five basic classes of people in your society.

At the top of your society was the king and his family.

Next came the nobles and important landholders. Even though you were not noble, this was the class in which your family belonged. If you went back in history, one of your ancestors was related to a duke. The king granted land to these people, and in return, they had to provide soldiers to help defend the country. Your father had to swear an oath of loyalty to the king and become his vassal, which meant he served the king. Sometimes he granted them a title, elevating them to the noble class.

Your father had many knights or soldiers that made their home with you. They were the backbone of the army. They swore fealty (feel-tee) to your father, giving him the manpower to help the king. They rarely owned land unless they were rewarded for something they did in battle like your father.

The clergy were the priests and nuns. Many wealthy people sent at least one of their children to join the church. They usually ended up in a position of great power. The churches were important to society. Priests were the only people who could read the Bible and explain it to common people.

All children were baptized and everyone went to church on Sunday. Mass was in Latin, and most people did not understand a word of the prayers.

Church was also the place you went to when someone got sick. The priests and nuns knew how to use medicines to heal people. The church had an almonry (al-lun-ree) where food and money were given to the poor, an infirmary (in-firm-a-ree) where they took care of the sick.

They could also stay with a hospitaller (hos-pit-al-er) where knights housed travelers visiting religious shrines that were found all over England.

People went on spiritual pilgrimages, walking long distances to see holy relics and pray to the saint associated with these shrines. A holy relic was physical remains or something the saint had owned or touched. Often you heard of a miracle happening like a wish coming true or a healing. The journey was hard and tested the faith of the travelers. Staying with a hospitaller was a safe place to rest and gather their strength.

At the bottom of society were the peasants. Most of them were serfs or villeins (vil-leins). The un-free ones were a little more than slaves and couldn't leave the land without your father's permission. They had to farm your father's land for two days a week, as well as work extra days during busy times like the harvest. Some of them had to pay rent to farm the small plots of land they rented from your father. They had a very hard life.

They had to turn over their best animal when the head of the household died before a son could take over a father's land.

They had to grind their flour in your father's mill and give a portion of their grain as payment.

Freemen didn't have it much better, but they could leave when they wanted to and they could carry a weapon.

Peasants lived in simple huts. A wooden frame was built and filled in with a plaster of animal hair and clay called wattle (watt-l) and daub (dub), which were sticks, clay, and animal hair used in the wooden walls. Sometimes they were whitewashed or painted in bright colors. The poorest had one room; more prosperous could have larger huts with two rooms. They had a small window that had a shutter to keep out the bad weather.

There was no chimney, so the hearth was in the center of the hard packed earth floor. It was used for cooking and heating. The floor was covered with straw for warmth.

Part of the hut was walled off for animals.

People slept on the floor and used a log as a pillow. There was a rough wooden table and a few benches. Rush torches dipped in animal fat gave the dimly lit interior it's only light. It was smoky and smelly.

Tools and pottery hung from hooks. The family ate from wooden bowls.

The children of the poor had more choice of who they could marry, but their lives were filled with hard work.

They started as young as five, chasing away birds from the crops; the work getting harder as they grew older.

Most peasants owned a few chickens, goats, sheep, pigs, and perhaps a cow.

By the winter, they had to slaughter their livestock because they needed the food and didn't have enough feed to keep them alive for the cold months. The meat was salted and preserved.

A peasant woman's life was filled with endless hours of hard work. They washed clothes, spun wool, cooked, farmed alongside their husbands, took care of the children, brewed ale, milked the cows, made cheese, and baked bread; the day was endless. They had lots of children.

They worked from dawn til dusk.

Things were changing for females. You had heard of women in the towns and villages that were running businesses if their husbands died.

A tinker who brought ribbons and fixed pots and pans from his wagon told of a woman in the next town who ran a brewery. She was working and earning enough money to support herself.

A woman was expected to know how to run a business if her husband took ill or was away fighting. If anything terrible happened to him, the family would make her remarry someone else to take care of her. You would never have as much freedom as that woman the tinker talked about in the other town.

You dreamed of going to visit a town. The cities were filled with all kinds of shops. You heard that London was dirty and smelly but a thrilling place to visit.

There were barrel-makers called coopers, dyers, potters, and fullers who cleaned the wool before it was dyed. Fletchers who made arrows, butchers, bakers, carpenters and blacksmiths were ways to earn a living. There were so many different trades a person could learn.

Children would be apprenticed at seven-years-old to one of these tradesmen. Their fathers would pay a fee for them to learn a craft. They had to move in with the family and work long hours without getting paid for many years before it was decided they were qualified.

Craftsmen and their families lived in the back of their shops. They all belonged to guilds which were organized groups that fixed prices and made rules about the amount of hours they could work.

If you got sick, your parents called in a doctor from the village. He studied the ancient books of Galen (Gay-len), who practiced medicine in the years 130 to about 200 AD. Medicine hadn't changed much in a thousand years. The doctors believed that a body was filled with four substances called humors (hu-mers). These fluids defined a person's personality and their behavior. When they were in balance, a person was healthy. All diseases were caused when there was too much of one and not enough of another. They told you that illness came because you breathed bad vapors in the air.

The four humors were black bile, yellow bile, phlegm (flem), and blood. These were the liquids found in your body and used for diagnosis. They were referred to as: choler, phlegm, melancholy (mel-lon-ko-lee), and blood. Doctors said that each was related to your mood.

If a person had too much yellow bile, they were choleric (col-lar-ic) and quick to anger. If they had too much black bile, they were melancholy and sad.

The solution was usually to do a blood-letting. They would cut a patient on their forearm and let the bad blood drain from the body, allowing the good blood to rebalance their humors.

You hated when they did that to you because it left you weak for months. You much prefered to let Old Edith, the midwife give you herbs instead. She delivered all the babies, and you thought she knew more than any old doctor.

Doctors also depended on zodiac signs and the positions of the planet to figure out your health.

Most doctors attended a university, but apothecaries were the ones to prepare and dispense medicine.

Doctors were expensive and people didn't have much money. Many operations were done by barber-surgeons. People traveled to villages looking for shops with a white pole that had used bandages hanging from it. The white pole represented a tool that people held in their hand during procedures and the bloody bandages were there to clean up the mess.

Some shops painted a white pole with red stripes outside their door, representing the bloody bandages for their customers who couldn't read. People liked this cheaper alternative to doctors for surgery and pulling out teeth.

You could also get a shave and a haircut there as well.

Your parents used the minted coins marked as sterling silver to pay for the doctor's services.

Your father had an income of about three thousand pounds a year. Most people made a few pennies per day, so that made your family rather rich.

The term pound represented one pound of silver coin. Most people never used pounds but mostly shillings and pennies.

You were never bored. Your father and older brothers often hunted deer. They had a pack of dogs that searched out game. They killed the wild boars that roamed the countryside using long spears.

Once in a great while, they took you hawking. Your father had a beautiful falcon that captured pheasants and rabbits. He trained the bird to hunt small animals and bring them back to him.

Tournaments had to be your favorite activity. They usually lasted four days! Large crowds came from all over to watch the knights test their courage and skill with archery, jousting, and sword fights.

There were wrestling matches, cock-fighting between roosters, and bear-baiting. You were not allowed to attend these bloody sports, but you knew your little brother snuck out to watch.

There was lots of food, singing, and merry dancing! Everyone from peasant to lord had a good time.

In the evenings, there were feasts, dancing, and lots of games to play like chess and backgammon (back-gam-on), a strange game from the Middle East.

Minstrels or bands of wandering musicians passed through playing flutes and lutes, as well as other stringed instruments like mandores (man-dors) and dulcimers (dul-sem-ers). They sang love songs they learned in the famous courts from all over the continent of Europe.

In the winter, your father fashioned skates from a cow's shoulder blade, and you and your sisters skated on the pond outside your home.

You knew the church was a major part of your life. You were taught to pray many times throughout the day.

Your father said the church was more powerful than the king. The king had to adhere to the rules or he could be excommunicated, and that was heresy. Sometimes the king and the pope, who was head of the church disagreed. It created a lot of trouble and usually the pope won the argument.

The church had its own laws and collected taxes. Going against the churches rules and beliefs was considered heresy.

There were great cathedrals being built throughout many cities in Europe. It would take a hundred years to complete these giant buildings.

Most of them were built in the shape of a cross. They were filled with beautiful tapestries and jewel-like colored glass windows with scenes from the Bible.

Your step-mother had talked about the soaring ceilings with beautiful and dramatic arches and naves in the gothic style. They were a testimony to man's ability and skill to create wondrous things.

You would have loved to go to one, but chances were you never would be able to travel further than the next castle.

You never traveled far. Roads were dangerous and full of bandits.

Men rode on horseback, and your step-mother traveled in a wagon covered with painted cloth. She told you it was bumpy and uncomfortable. They couldn't go fast.

It was much better to travel by water, using the many rivers or the open sea. They went by a boat with one sail called a cog. It was faster, safer, and less expensive.

No matter how much you wanted to learn what your brothers were taught, your parents told you girls did not go to school. Your step-mother did teach you how to read. You loved the beautiful and expensive romances she had in her collection of books from France. They were each handwritten and rare.

You knew that sometimes a priest would educate some of the poor children to read and write. Boys from middle class families were allowed to attend grammar schools.

Grammar schools were run by priests involved with the bigger cathedrals. Not many could attend; the hours were long, and discipline was severe. Students were beaten with birch rods when they didn't answer correctly.

Smart students went to further their education in a university where they learned rhetoric, grammar, logic, arithmetic, music, medicine, and geometry. Many times they had to travel all the way to Paris, Italy, or Spain to find a school. You knew of a neighbor whose son was in Salerno (Sa-lare-no) where he studied medicine with foreign teachers.

One of your female cousins was allowed to go to a school in a convent. There she learned to read the Bible. The nuns taught her how to grow special herbs to heal people. She was smart, but your parents did not want to send you away.

So you see, if you were me, how life in the Middle Ages could really be.

Famous People from the Middle Ages

William the Conqueror- William I (Will-yum)- (c-1028-1087)- was the first Norman King of England. He was he Duke of Normandy and the descendant of Viking raiders. He launched an invasion of England in 1066, successfully winning the throne to rule England.

Hildegard of Bingen (Hil-dee-gard of Bing-in)- (1098-1179)- also known as Saint Hildegard. She was a German abbess, writer, composer, and philosopher. She was considered to be the founder of the scientific natural history in Germany.

Clovis (Clo-vis)- (c. 466-c.511)- first king of the Franks to unite all the tribes under one ruler. He is the founder of the Merovingian (Mer-ov-ee-an) dynasty which ruled the Frankish kingdom for the next two hundred years.

Joan of Arc (Jean de Arc)- (c-1412-1431)- also known as the Maid of Orleans (Or-leans). Joan was a peasant girl who had a vision instructing her to support Charles VII and make the English leave France during the Hundred Years' War. Her bravery boosted the morale of the soldiers, earning them several victories. Later, she was arrested by the English and burned at the stake for heresy.

Saladin An-Nasir Yusuf ibn Ayyub (Sal-a-din An Na-seer You-sef ibn- Ay-yub) (1137-1193) was the first sultan or leader of Egypt and Syria and the founder of the Ayyubid dynasty (Ay-yu-bid). He led the Muslim army against the Crusader troops in the Middle East.

Bede (Beed)- (c.672-735)- was known as Saint Bede or the Venerable Bede. He was an English monk at a monastery in England. He was a famous author and scholar. His most famous book about the history of the English people gave him the title "The Father of English History."

Eleanor of Aquitaine (El-leon-nor of A-qua-taine)- (c 1122-1204) - one of the wealthiest and most powerful women in western Europe during the Middle Ages. She married the king of France, later divorcing him to become Queen of England when she married Henry II. She was famous for her love of art and literature.

Christine de Pizan (Chris-tee-na de Piz-an)- (1364- c.1430)- a famous noblewoman who wrote biographies, poetry, and books containing practical ideas for women. She completed forty-one books. She also recorded court life for French dukes.

Charlemagne (Char-lee-mayne)- (c748-814)- also known as Charles the Great or Charles I. He united most of Western Europe during the Middle Ages. He was the first Holy Roman Emperor, the first recognized emperor since the fall of the Roman Empire three hundred years earlier.

Glossary

Aalis (A-lish)- a popular girl's name in the Middle Ages.

abbess (a-biss)- a woman who is the head nun in a abbey.

ale (aye-l)- a type of beer with a fruity taste.

almonry (al-mun-ree)- a building where the distribution of money and food were given to poor people.

amber (am-burr)- a fossil-like tree resin with a yellowish-brown color. Amber is often used for jewelry.

apothecaries (a-poth-a-carries)- one who supplies and distributes medicine.

apprentice (ah-pren-tis)- someone who is obligated to work under a tradesmen to learn their craft for a few years without pay until it was decided that the apprentice was experienced enough to receive pay.

Arras (Ar-rahs)- a rich fabric that is weaved together by hand creating a design in the material, used to cover furniture or to hang on the wall. A region in France where tapestries are made.

archer (arch-er)- a person with the skills of using a bow and arrow.

archery (arch-ary)- the skill to shoot a bow and arrow.

armor-(ar-mer)- the metal coverings worn by knights to protect them in battle.

baptize (bap-tyze)- when someone is immersed in water to be accepted into a religion.

backgammon (back-gam-on)- a board game where two players take turns rolling the dice and moving their chips around as well as off the board.

barber-surgeon (bar-ber-sur-jun)- a doctor who handled all kinds of small operations using their many sharp tools like razors and knives.

bailey (bail-lee)- the outer wall of a castle, usually enclosing a courtyard.

barbette (bar-bet)- a headdress worn over the hair with a chin strip.

bear-baiting (bear-bay-ting)- a sort of blood-sport of having dogs attack a chained up bear.

birch rods (ber-ch rods)- a flexible twig or several twigs from a birch tree used to hit a person for punishment.

blacksmith (blak-smith)- a person who creates tools and horseshoes in a forge.

blanchette (blanch-et)- a white woolen blanket.

blood (blaud)- part of the four body fluids that defined human personality types and behavior. Blood or sanguine (san-qwine) often described a cheery and hopeful person.

blood-letting (blaud-letting)- a popular treatment for illness. Doctors would cut a person on the arm or leg and allow the "bad blood" that was making them ill leave the body.

boars (bors)- wild pigs.

braiel (bray-el)- a belt strap.

braies (bray-es)- a type of linen underwear.

brewery (broo-a-ree)- a place where beer is made.

brooch (bro-ch)- a decorative piece of jewelry worn pinned to clothing.

buttery (but-uh-ree)- the room where all the barrels of wine and ale are stored.

carp (karp)- a freshwater fish.

cathedrals (kath-ed-rels)- the prime Catholic Church closely associated with the priest and the bishop.

Catholic (Cath-o-lik)- belonging to the Catholic Church or Church of Rome.

chapel (chap-el)- a part of a house or building dedicated to religion and prayer.

chaplet (chap-let)- a wreath of flowers worn in the hair.

choler (col-ar)- anger and bad temper that was represented by yellow bile when the body has too much off balance.

choleric (col-lar-ic)- the act of getting annoyed and angered easily.

church (cher-ch)- a place of Christian worship for the public.

clergy (kler-je)- people appointed by the church to do religious duties.

cloak (klok)- outer garment without sleeves worn over clothing.

cock-fighting (kok-fighting)- people pit roosters against each other in a fight used as entertainment.

cogs (kogs)- a ship made out of oak timber with a single mast, widely used for sea-trade.

convent (con-vint)- a Christian school for girls under religious vows, notably for nuns.

cooper (koop-er)- to make or repair barrels or casks.

cowl (koul)- a large, loose hood worn on the head.

craftsman (crafts-man)- a person who creates useful or beautiful objects.

crenellate (kren-el-late)- building fortifications on the top of a building.

crossbow (cros-bow)- a horizontal bow-like weapon that shoots bolt-like arrows.

Crusader (Kroo-sae-der)- a soldier dedicated to fight for his religion.

Crusades (Kroo-saeds)- a series of wars called by the popes against the enemies of the church and the battle of property in the Holy Land.

daub (dawb)- plaster, clay, or another substance used for coating a surface, especially when mixed with straw to form a wall.

demesne (dea-meyn)- the part of land on a large estate for the owner's use.

diagnosis (di-ag-nos-is)- identifying an illness.

dais (day-us)- a raised platform where the head table is placed for important people to be seen while they eat.

divorce (de-vorce)- a legal action taken to end a marriage.

dovecote (dov-cote)- a tower where doves nest.

dubbed (dub-ed)- to be given an official name and recognized.

duke (duk)- the highest title in nobility.

dulcimers (dul-sem-ers)- a trapezoid shaped musical instrument with strings that is played by hitting the strings with a handheld hammer or by plucking and strumming.

dynasty (di-ne-stee)- a family of rulers who rule over a country for a long period of time.

Edith (Ee-dith)- a popular girl's name in the Middle Ages.

Egypt (E-gipt)- a country that borders the Mediterranean and Red Seas which is Northeast of Africa.

Europe (Ur-up)- a continent in the middle of Asia and the Atlantic within the eastern hemisphere.

excommunicated (ex-come-un-ikated)- when a person is told they cannot participate in church rituals.

falcon (fal-ken)- a raptor type of bird.

fealty (feel-tee)- an obligation to be loyal.

feast (fest)- a large, rich meal. A feast usually takes place for a special occasion or celebration with many people.

feudal (few-dal)- farmers worked land in exchange for services and protection from an overlord.

feed (feed)- food given to animals.

feudalism (few-dal-ism)- a social system in Europe during the Middle Ages in which people worked and fought for landowners who gave them protection and the use of land in return.

fiefdom (feef-doms)- the estate of a feudal lord.

fleece (flee-s)- the wooly skin on a sheep or goat.

fletchers (flech-ers)- a person who makes arrows.

foster (fos-ter)- bringing up a child not their own.

Frankish (Frank-ish)- the name for the early French people.

fullers (full-ers)- a person who cleans the wool before it is dyed a color.

Galen (Gay-len)- Claudius Galenus (September 129 AD – c. 200/c. 216)- a Greek doctor whose books became the foundation for doctors in the Middle Ages.

garderobe (gar-ter robe)- a toilet in a Medieval castle was often a hole in the stone of the tower that let waste fall into the moat.

Geoffrey (Jef-free)- a popular boy's name in the Middle Ages.

gothic style (goth-ik)- a popular style of architecture during the Middle Ages with large windows, pointed arches, and elaborate decorations.

grammar schools (gram-ar)- a school usually attached to a cathedral or church where young boys started their education.

hauberk (ho-berk)- the tiny loops of metal woven into a long shirt of armor.

hawking (hok-ing)- a sport using a trained falcon to hunt for small animals.

hearth (harth)- the flooring of a fireplace.

heresy (her-re-see)- having a belief that is contrary to that of the church's doctrine.

heron (her-un)- a large, white stork-like bird with a long neck, bill, and legs.

Holy Land (Ho-lee Land)- the countries in the Middle East, like Palestine, where it is believed by Christians that Jesus Christ lived there.

holy relic (ho-lee re-lik)- the physical remains or personal belonging of a saint or important person kept in a memorial in a church for people to visit.

Holy Roman Emperor (Ho-lee Row-man Em-per-er)- many European areas that the Frankish or German king ruled. The king who ruled during that time gained the title of Roman Emperor.

hospitaller (hos-pit-al-er)- the Crusader knights that protected religious pilgrims when they traveled to visit Holy sites. They provided meals, a place to sleep, protection, and medical aide.

humors (hu-mers)- the four fluids in the human body that define personality type and behavior.

infirmary (in-firm-a-ree)- a hospital run by monks or Crusader knights.

jousting (jowst-ing)- a contest when to knights fight each other with lances.

keep (keep)- a fortified tower in a castle.

knight (nite)- a warrior who served his liege or leader as an armored soldier.

Latin (Lat-in)- the official language of the Catholic Church.

liege (lee-je)- a lord or leader.

linen (lin-en)- a fabric made out of flax yarn used to create bedding, clothes, tablecloths, and more.

logic (loge-ik)- reasonable thinking.

London (Lun-dun)- the capital of England.

lute (loot)- a the stringed instrument.

mandore (man-dor)- a tear-dropped shaped, small string instrument.

manor (man-er)- a big house on a vast amount of land.

mantle (man-tl)- a men's cloak that was worn over the shoulder.

Mass (Mass)- the church service.

mead (medd)- an ale-like drink flavored with honey.

Medieval (Mid-e-vil)- the time period during the one thousand years in Europe from the 400s to 1400s within the Middle Ages.

melancholy (mel-lon-ko-lee)- one of the four body fluids that described the four humors of the body determining behavior and personality. This is represented by black bile and indicated sadness.

Melisende (Me-le-sand)- a popular girl's name in the Middle Ages.

midwife (mid-wyf)- a trained medicine woman who helped deliver babies.

millennium (mil-len-ni-um)- a period of a thousand years.

minstrels (min-stru-hls)- a band of musicians that usually traveled from town to town earning money by performing in the manor houses.

miracle (mir-a-cle)- a surprising event not explainable by science or nature.

moat (mot)- a deep ditch surrounding a castle, sometimes filled with water.

monk (monk)- a deeply religious person who dedicates himself to serving others as well as a life of prayers and meditation.

motte (mott)- a hill on which a castle is built.

Muslim (Mus-lim)- a person who follows the religion of Islam.

mutton (mut-ton)- meat of domestic sheep.

naves (naves)- central part of the church that holds the congregation.

noble (no-bel)- belonging to the highest social class; of relating to or belonging to the nobility.

Normandy (Nor-man-de)- a region on the coast of France. The name Normandy originated from the Normans also known as the northmen who settled in the region.

Norsemen (Nors-men)- means "men from the north," referred to people from Scandinavia.

nun (nen)- women who join the Catholic church dedicating their lives to prayer and serving others.

page (page)- usually a seven year old's first job as an attendant to a knight, where he will learn courtly manners.

patten (pat-ten)- a wooden clog worn over shoes outdoors for mud.

peasants (pez-uhnts)- a poor farmer.

pennies (pen-ees)- currency.

philosopher (fil-o-so-fer)- a person who studies culture and why people do the things they do.

phlegm (flem)- one of the four body fluids used to determine behavior and personaity.

Phlegm determines peaceful and relaxed.

pike (pie-k)- a freshwater fish.

pilgrimage (pil-grim-age)- a religious journey.

pope (po-puh)- the head of the Catholic Church.

portcullis (port-a-cu-lus)- a heavy iron and wood gate that protects a castle.

pottage (pot-ige)- a soup or stew usually made out of vegetables and meat.

potter (pot-ter)- someone who molds and creates pottery like bowls and plates out of clay.

pounds (pounds)- currency.

preserve (pre-serve)- prepare (fruit, vegetables, etc.) by cooking or smoking with sugar or pickling for long-term storage without spoiling.

priest (pree-st)- someone in the clergy who dedicates his life to serving others. Renais-

sance (Ren-ai-san-ce)- the European historical time period from the 14th through the 17th century which focuses on the new found interests of science, ancient art, and literature.

rhetoric (ret-or-ik)- great command of language and words to persuade people to a point of view.

Rouen (Ro-yhn)- a town in France.

Roul (Ro-ul)- a popular boys name in the Middle Ages.

rush (rush)- the straw used to sop up dirt on the floor.

rural (roo-el)- from the countryside.

saint (saynt)- one who is accepted by the church as a holy person.

Salerno (Sa-lare-no)- a city in Italy with a great university.

scallop (ska-loop)- a curved ornamental border.

Scandinavia (Skan-dun-a-via)- a large peninsula in northwestern Europe, occupied by Norway and Sweden.

scholars (skal-ers)- a student who has studied a particular subject and has deep knowledge on said subject.

serfs (ser-fs)- a slave.

shift (shift)- a simple kind of undergarment like a slip.

shillings (shil-lings)- currency.

shrines (sh-rines)- a place that people visit because it is connected with someone or something that is important to them.

solar (so-ler)- a room meant for the lord and ladies of the castle to sleep. The room also provided a private space for the lord's family to sit and talk.

spit (spit)- a pole hung in a fireplace for roasting meat.

squire (skw-ire)- a young nobleman who attends a knight as training to be a knight himself.

standard bearer (stan-derd bear-er)- a soldier who is responsible for carrying the flag of an army.

Syria (Sear-ee-uh)- a country in Southwest Asia in the Middle East.

tallow (tal-low)- hard substance created from melted animal fat and made into soap and candles.

tapestries (ta-pes-trees)- the woven rugs hung on walls for decoration and warmth.

taxes (taks-es)- money each citizen and business is required to pay to the government to help pay for community services and facilities such as parks, budgeting for school, free health clinics, church and temple budgets, and more.

tradesman (tray-ds-man)- one who has an occupation in a learned job such as a shoemaker or baker.

Theobald (Thee-o-bald)- a popular boy's name in the Middle Ages.

tinker (tin-ker)- a person who travels from place to place fixing household items.

tiltyard (tilt-yard)- an area where jousts take place.

tournaments (torn-a-ments)- a competition where many knight came to compete in various sports or games to see who was the most skilled and bravest.

translucent (trans-loo-cent)- allowing light but not detailed images.

trencher (tren-chur)- the bread used as a platter.

trousers (trou-zers)- pants, usually worn by men.

tunic (too-nick)- a loose piece of clothing usually without sleeves that reaches to the knees and worn by men and women.

turnbrocie (turn-bro-cee)- a servant who turned the roasting mean on a spit in a fireplace.

vapors (vay-pers)- a substance in the air, like a cloud.

vassal (vass-uhl)- a person who received protection and land from a lord in return for loyalty and service.

Viking (Vyk-ing)- Scandinavian pirates who raided and settled in parts of northwestern Europe in the 8th–11th centuries.

villeins (vil-leins)- a feudal serf subject to a lord or manor to whom he paid dues and services in return for land.

warlord (war-lord)- a military leader.

wattle (wat-tel)- the material for making fences, walls, etc., consisting of rods or stakes interlaced with twigs or branches.

whitewashed (white-wash-ed)- a blend of lime and water usually with other substances used to whiten walls.

zodiac (zoh-di-ack)- a map of the stars that is represented by twelve signs. Doctors used those signs to determine a person's health.

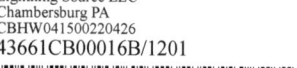